AT THE RIM

Marlene Karas

*A Celebration of
Women's Collegiate
Basketball*

One for all and all for one: Georgia players pull into a tight huddle during their game with Iowa in the SEC/Big Ten Challenge.

Mary Schroeder

Marthea McCloud of Kansas runs on court as the announcer introduces her before a game with Missouri.

(Overleaf) Virginia's Tammi Reiss dribbles downcourt in the ACC semifinal game, guarded by Courtney Johnson of Clemson.

Mary Schroeder

Rebecca Barger

Washington Husky
teammates celebrate
their victory over Stan-
ford just after one of
their players captured
a loose ball and made
the winning basket.

Meri Simon

AT THE RIM

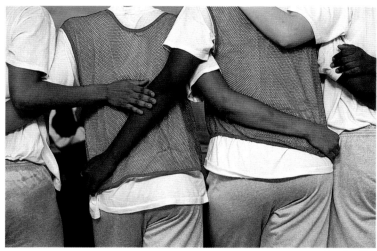

Pam Spaulding

A Celebration of Women's Collegiate Basketball

Introduction by Patsy Neal

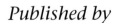

Published by

Professional Photography Division,
Eastman Kodak Company

and

Thomasson-Grant

(This page) After Notre Dame's win over
St. Joseph's in the St. Joseph's Tournament,
head coach Muffet McGraw (far left) smiles
at her six-month-old son as he crawls past his
mother's winning team.

(Previous two pages)
Kelly Dougherty of Stanford warms up during half time
in a game with the University of Washington.

Tennessee players form a huddle during a morning
practice session at the Super Shootout in Hilton Head.

Published by the Professional Photography Division,
Eastman Kodak Company and Thomasson-Grant

Designed by Lisa Lytton-Smith
Editing, profiles, and captions by Rebecca Beall Barns
Photography edited by Susan Vermazen
Photography coordinated by Sam Abell and
Leah Painter Roberts

Introduction © copyright 1991 Patsy Neal.
Foreword © copyright 1991 Betty F. Jaynes.

Printed and bound in U.S.A. by Progress Printing.

98 97 96 95 94 93 92 91 5 4 3 2 1

Library of Congress Cataloging-in-Publication Data

At the rim: a celebration of women's collegiate basketball /
     introduction by Patsy Neal.
         p.   cm.
     ISBN 0-934738-91-2
          1. Basketball for women--United States--History.
     2. College sports--United States--History. 3. Women
     basketball players--United States--Biography. I. East-
     man Kodak Company. Professional Photography
     Division.
     GV886.A8   1991
     796.323'8--dc20   91-18213
                                                   CIP

Thomasson-Grant, Inc.
One Morton Drive, Suite 500
Charlottesville, VA 22901
(804) 977-1780

Vicki Valerio

THE PHOTOGRAPHERS

Jeanie Adams

Amanda L. Alcock

Donna Bagby

Ellen M. Banner

Rebecca Barger

Nicole Bengiveno

Lois Bernstein

Susan Biddle

Paula Bronstein

Christine Cotter

Dana Fineman

Pat Greenhouse

Judy Griesedieck

Reneé Hannans

Adrienne Helitzer

Lynn Johnson

Marlene Karas

Pauline Lubens

Paula Nelson

Mary Schroeder

Mary E. Schulte

Callie Shell

Jean Shifrin

Laura Sikes

Meri Simon

Pam Spaulding

Barbara M. Trammell

Vicki Valerio

Lisa Waddell-Buser

Cindy Yamanaka

Forward Lisa Sandbothe of the
University of Missouri concentrates
on a foul shot in a game with Kansas.

Alexis Rinaldo collects balls for Rutgers players at practice before the Bell Atlantic Tournament in New Brunswick, New Jersey.

Nicole Bengiveno

I KEPT HEARING the thud of a basketball on the concrete floor outside as I was trying to give a coaching clinic at the YWCA in Santa Monica. The sound was invasive. It echoed through the classroom, and I saw more than one attendee looking toward the door in annoyance. Yet it was this very reverberation that brought these coaches to sit in my classroom on a balmy Saturday afternoon. The perpetrator: nine-year-old Lara Hanson. In a cut-off T-shirt and high tops she stood impatiently outside our classroom, bouncing the ball, attempting to pass it between those skinny legs, her ponytail swaying in the stillness of the hall-way. No gym, no hoop, just a girl and a ball, waiting to be coached.

I said to her, "What are you doing?" She said, "I'm waiting for my dad. He's taking your class." I said, "Are you a basketball player?" She said, "Yeah, I am." Not "I will be," but "I am."

Until recent years, young girls' ideas of basketball were fueled mostly by stories of the men who played the game. Girls could only dream of their own heroes, and the stars of women's national championships stood by and watched while men were lauded and sought after for scholarships and endorsements. The women's teams were cheered by more good intentions than fans. So we kept our visions to ourselves, pursued them on our own courts, and waited until the world was ready for them.

It is ready for them now, and my hope is that this book of photographs will be a book of heroes for the Laras of the world.

Betty F. Jaynes
Executive Director,
Women's Basketball Coaches Association

Photo by Adrienne Helitzer

Penn State's Tanya Garner dribbles down-court in a game against St. Joseph's in the Atlantic Ten Conference Tournament.

I **WAS ONE** of the lucky ones. Growing up in Georgia, one of the few states that offered women competitive sports in high school in the 1950s, I lived in a small spot of light during the dark ages of women's basketball. I still remember dreading high school graduation because I could not conceive of life without the game. By a miracle, I saw a two-line paragraph in a paper I seldom read, announcing that Wayland College in Plainview, Texas, had won the women's AAU National Basketball Championship. Chills ran over my body as I read those two lines over and over.

Patsy Neal (left) accepts flowers as captain of the U.S. team at the 1964 World Basketball Tournament in Lima, Peru.

I immediately wrote Wayland requesting a tryout, and my parents, at their own expense, drove me to Texas. I was scared to death—not of failure—but of losing the opportunity to extend my being through the bouncing of a leather ball.

I came away from the tryout with a full basketball scholarship, and my life was never the same. Even today, the smell of leather makes me feel more alive. Sometimes I wonder where I would be now if I had not seen that two-line paragraph in the paper. But here I am, writing to tell others of the magic of basketball.

How can I describe the pride of carrying the U.S. flag before 30,000 spectators in a foreign country, or the chills that still run up my spine every time I hear the national anthem? What words could possibly tell someone what it feels like to soar through the air to snag a rebound off the board? Who could ever explain how marvelous it is to get a second wind when your legs are dragging and your lungs are about to explode?

Athletes are blessed creatures, capable of performing with impressive power and grace. In the process of competition, the intricate connections between mind and body are defined by a spirit that refuses to acknowledge the limits of ordinary people. As we play, records are set and broken, and some athletes are fortunate enough to be remembered for all time.

Senda Berenson (center, in long skirt) tosses a jump ball in a match played at Smith College in 1906.

These women of the class of 1895 won the first intramural women's basketball game, played at Smith College in 1893.

We are in the golden age of women's basketball, and I am thrilled for the women who have the opportunity to compete today. At the same time, I am sad for the many fine athletes and coaches of the past who struggled and fought for every bit of competition they could find. Some of the finest players that ever walked on a court are unheard of simply because they lived and played before Title IX.

Out of fairness to all the women who blazed the way to these golden years, we must remember that basketball did not start in the seventies when media coverage made the game more visible to the public. Women's basketball started in the late 1800s, and some of its best days may have been in the fifties and sixties.

Senda Berenson of Smith College organized the first known women's basketball teams in 1892, just three months after James Naismith first tacked a peach basket up in a YMCA gym in Springfield, Massachusetts. From the very beginning of women's basketball, she greatly influenced the direction of women's rules. Even so, like most physical educators of her day, she was against intercollegiate competition for women.

The first known women's basketball game between two colleges was on April 4, 1896, between Stanford and the University of California, Berkeley. The Berkeley women agreed to play under two conditions: the game had to be played indoors, and no men would be allowed to watch. It was reported that when two men had to come in to prop up a basket, "the Berkeley team screamed and hid in a corner."

When the screaming was over and the basket repaired, the game continued. In a great scoring contest, Stanford beat Berkeley 2-1. Offense has obviously improved since then. On January 12, 1991, Virginia defeated North Carolina State 123-120 in three overtimes to set a new record for the total number of points scored in a women's basketball game, as well as for the number of points scored by a losing team. We do not know how many spectators watched the first game between Stanford and Berkeley, but 11,520 were present to watch Virginia and N.C. State.

Not only has offense changed, but so have the rules. In 1899, a committee led by Senda Berenson "officially" adopted the six-player, three-court game, and Spalding published the rules. Still, many different versions of the rules continued to be played. The two-court game was officially adopted in 1938, with three stationary guards and three stationary forwards. In the fifties

and early sixties, the "roving" game was used, with two stationary forwards, two stationary guards, and two players who could cover the whole court playing offense and defense as "rovers."

The Flying Queens, National AAU Champions of the 1957-58 season, pose in front of one of four Beechcraft Bonanzas that ferried them to games. Author Patsy Neal is seventh from left.

The rules changed to become more and more like the men's until finally, after much controversy, the five-player game was used on an experimental basis during the 1969-70 season and officially adopted in 1970. Those who fought the change wanted to keep the unique "roving" game for a couple of reasons. While slower players could specialize in the roving game and still participate as stationary guards or forwards, the faster, full-court game eliminated all players but the most highly skilled. In addition, educators weren't sure that women were physically able to play the more strenuous full-court game.

From its beginning in 1892, women's basketball had spread quickly. By 1920, it was played on every continent, but was held back in the United States by physical educators who were against intercollegiate competition for women because it was considered unfeminine.

Recognizing the need to provide competitive opportunities for women, the Amateur Athletic Union (AAU) as early as 1926 had organized the first National Women's Basketball Championship in Los Angeles, California. The first national championship was played under men's rules, but by 1937, the AAU had published its own rules. By 1929, the AAU National Championship had become an annual event which continues even today.

In the 1920s, the first well-known woman player, "Babe" Didrikson, played for a basketball team called the Golden Cyclones, scoring 106 points in five games to lead her team to the 1931 AAU Championship. Her coach, Colonel Melvorne McCombs, dispensed with the baggy bloomers and loose-fitting blouses worn by women competitors at that time in favor of blue shorts and white jerseys. The Cyclones later switched to orange satin shorts, not only increasing ticket sales, but starting a new fad in uniforms for women athletes. (The Pasadena Athletic and Country Club basketball team may have actually been first to give up bloomers, in 1925.)

It was not until World War II that women's basketball began to grow rapidly. Most educators in the thirties and forties limited competition for women to "play days," an informal and social form of competition in which players from different schools engaged in a variety of sports, with little emphasis on winning. But as women entered the work force to replace men

In the late fifties and early sixties, Wayland College, shown here in competition with the Raytown Piperettes, played 131 straight games without defeat.

who had gone to war, industrial leagues for women sprang up.

It has been estimated that at one time there were more than 10,000 companies sponsoring sports programs (including basketball) for women. Hanes, an industrial team from Winston-Salem, North Carolina, became famous as they won three straight national championships (1951-1953) and ran up a winning streak of 102 games. "Eckie" Jordan, a five-time All-American for Hanes Hosiery, summed up the feelings of most women players in the forties and fifties: "I would have gone to the moon to play in a basketball game." AAU women's basketball was strengthened greatly by the teams coming from industries.

During the fifties and sixties, two colleges, Wayland College of Plainview, Texas, and Nashville Business College in Tennessee, pioneered women's collegiate basketball. Wayland, far ahead of the times, offered full basketball scholarships to women in the early fifties, more than 20 years before Title IX. The sponsor of Wayland's team, a Plainview businessman named Claude Hutcherson, flew the team to all their games in four Beechcraft Bonanzas. After Hutcherson's death in 1977, his wife Wilda continued to sponsor the Queens.

The Hutcherson Flying Queens ran up a record that will probably never be broken by another college. They played 131 straight games without a defeat, won the National AAU Tournament 10 times, and finished second 9 times. They have placed 39 players on U.S. national teams, and have had players named to the All-American team 60 times. In February of 1988, Wayland won its thousandth game.

Wayland's main competitor, Nashville Business College, won 11 National AAU Championships, breaking Wayland's 131-game winning streak with a 46-42 win in the 1958 AAU National Championship game, and had 24 players who made the All-American team a total of 76 times. The amazing part of this record is that Nashville Business College won eight straight AAU Championships (1962-1969), winning 113 of their last 117 games. Unfortunately, NBC's program, started in 1924, ended in 1969 because its sponsor, H. O. Balls, did not want to go to the five-player game.

During the glory years of the fifties and sixties, Harley Redin coached Wayland, and John Head coached Nashville Business College. As shown by their records, these men were basketball geniuses. Redin coached the Queens for 18 years, running up a 431-66 win-loss record, and John Head coached at Nashville Business College for 23 years, winning 689 games while losing only 95, and establishing a streak of 96 straight wins in the mid-sixties. Both men were selected to coach U.S. All-Star teams after international women's basketball was sanctioned in 1953. John Head coached the U.S. teams to gold medals in the first and second World Basketball Championships (Santiago, Chile, in 1953 with 35,000 fans present, and Rio de Janeiro, Brazil, in 1957 before a crowd of 40,000). The U.S. team that played against the Russian All-Stars in the first women's basketball game in Madison Square Garden on November 26, 1959, was composed mainly of Wayland and Nashville Business College players.

Between 1956 and 1969, either John Head's or Harley Redin's team won the National AAU Championship. During the 14 years they coached against each other, they played each other 63 times. Wayland won 32 games, while Nashville Business College won 31. Their games were always electrifying, and fans would drive hundreds of miles to watch the two teams in action.

Nera White, a player for Nashville Business College, was probably the greatest woman basketball player who has ever lived. Few people have heard of her, though, because media coverage in the fifties and sixties was almost nonexistent for women. She made the All-American team 15 times, was named Most Valuable Player at the AAU Tournament 10 times, and was selected the best player in the world at the World Basketball Championship in 1957.

Players who competed against Nera, including myself, can tell you of feats that have not been matched even by present-day all-stars. Nera could shoot jump shots effortlessly and accurately from center court, as well as tip balls in from five to ten feet away from the basket. It was not unusual to see her leave the floor from the free-throw line and fly through the air for a lay-up shot, or cover the entire court in three dribbles. Her speed and wrist strength were amazing, considering that athletes of that time did not train with weights or use other modern techniques for conditioning. It is sad that her games were not filmed, and that her exceptional moves cannot be watched today.

I have often wondered how an all-star team from Wayland and Nashville Business College would have fared against the top players of today. Because of the limited number of college teams in the fifties and sixties, Wayland and Nashville Business College were able to draw the best players in the country, and their teams were powerful and dominating. The rivalry between Wayland and Nashville Business College was so intense that even today, more than 30 years later, I can replay highlights of our games in my mind.

By the late sixties, the "play day" concept was almost a thing of the past. Many colleges were providing competitive teams for women, and it became

Mullarky Studios

Moving with the speed that made her famous among players of her time, Nera White of Nashville Business College goes in for a two-handed lay-up.

Immaculata's Marianne Crawford Stanley drives for the basket in a game played against West Chester State College in 1974.

evident that women physical educators needed to be more active in women's sports programs. The DGWS (Division of Girls and Women's Sports) played a strong role in the development of rules and philosophy for women, followed later by the NAGWS (National Association of Girls and Women's Sports).

Finally, in 1969, the first National Intercollegiate Women's Basketball Tournament was held at West Chester State College in Pennsylvania. It was won by Immaculata College. The era of modern-day basketball had officially begun.

Fearing women would have the same problems that men were having in their programs, such as illegal recruiting and too much emphasis on winning, women physical educators formed the Association of Intercollegiate Athletics for Women (AIAW) in 1971. The AIAW's purpose was to sponsor national championships and sanction women's intercollegiate athletic events. For its first three years, the organization shunned basketball scholarships and recruiting in an attempt to keep the sport as free as possible of the pressure to win.

Women's sports got its biggest boost in 1972 when Congress passed Title IX. This law forced colleges receiving federal funds to be fairer to women in the budgeting of money, the recruitment of athletes, the rewarding of scholarships, the provision of advanced programs (including postseason championships), and coverage by the media.

As a result, the seventies saw a number of milestones in women's basketball:

In 1973, 11,000 fans watched Queens College play Immaculata College in Madison Square Garden.

Ann Meyers of UCLA signed with the Indiana Pacers to become the first woman drafted in the NBA.

The International Olympic Committee voted to add women's basketball to the 1976 Olympics in Montreal, and the American women won a silver medal.

The first poll of the nation's top 20 women's basketball teams was established by Mel Greenberg in 1976, published by the *Philadelphia Inquirer*, and picked up in 1978 by the Associated Press.

In 1977-78, NBC bought television rights to the women's basketball Division I Championships. The next year, NBC bought rights to all AIAW Division I National Championships, and ESPN purchased rights to show Division II and Division III National Championships.

The first Olympic competition for women in 1976 saw the Soviet Union beat the United States 112-77. This domination by the Soviet Union in women's basketball slowly diminished as the American women began to see results from Title IX and as better players began to come out of the increasingly competitive college programs.

With more media attention, attitudes toward women in sports began to change, and public support grew. Research pointed out that women were just as capable of strenuous exercise as men, and educators became more accepting of athletic competition as a positive experience for women.

In 1980, the women's basketball program was set back when President Carter decided that our teams would boycott the 1980 Olympics. The Russians again easily took the gold in the absence of the Americans, winning by 31 points over Bulgaria in the finals. But in 1982, the American women beat the Russians, posting an 85-83 win in Budapest. The U.S. beat the Soviet Union again in an exhibition game in Kansas City, 76-70, but lost two close games against them in the World Championship (these two losses came by a total of three points).

In 1984, Pat Head Summitt of the University of Tennessee coached the Americans to their first Olympic gold medal in women's basketball. In 1988, the U.S. won its second gold medal in Seoul, Korea. The U.S. coach, Kay Yow of N.C. State, used a relentless defense and aggressive fast breaks to defeat the Soviet Union 102-88 in the semifinals, and Yugoslavia 77-70 in the finals. The Russians were no longer able to intimidate the Americans, even though they had a 7'2", 260-pound, highly skilled center.

The 1980s saw many changes at the national level of women's basketball. In 1980-81, NBC televised ten women's sports national championships, and ESPN televised two. Corporate sponsorships such as the AIAW/Kodak All-America Basketball Team and the Broderick Cup (awarded annually to the most outstanding woman athlete) added to media coverage. The first NCAA National Women's Basketball Championship was held in 1982. In the mid-eighties, the women changed to a smaller, lighter ball, which made for faster passing and better shooting. In 1985, Lynette Woodard became the first woman selected to play with the Harlem Globetrotters.

Exultant players on the 1984 U.S. Olympic team carry coach Pat Head Summitt after defeating Korea 85-55 to win the nation's first Olympic gold medal in women's basketball.

USA Basketball

The U.S. Olympic Basketball team won the gold medal in 1988, defeating the Soviets in the semifinals 102-88 and Yugoslavia in the finals 77-70.

In the early 1980s, the AIAW, which had organized competition for women at the college level, was challenged by the NCAA. Consequently, in 1982, there were two National Basketball Championships for women. Most colleges chose to go with the NCAA, and 1981-82 was the last year for AIAW. Louisiana Tech won the first NCAA Division I Championship.

Many women found it hard to coach in the new, highly competitive atmosphere of women's athletics, and experienced men began to fill the open positions. There was a dramatic decline in leadership and in the number of coaching positions held by women in the 1970s and 1980s. Recently, however, there have been some encouraging signs as the NCAA has taken steps to increase the number of women in leadership. The most notable was the selection in 1991 of Judith Sweet, Athletic Director at San Diego University, as the first woman president of the NCAA.

Although the women's basketball championships had been televised before, 1991 was the first year that the NCAA signed a package deal with a network for the rights to broadcast three regular season games as well as the semifinals of the Division I Championship. Nora Lynn Finch, Associate Director of Athletics at N.C. State, feels that television is the key to the success of women's basketball. "We have come a long way, but we have a long way to go," she says. "The next hurdle is getting more television coverage." On February 23, 1991, a record 2.5 million viewers watched as CBS televised the University of Tennessee versus Texas game.

Today, women athletes find that they have many choices after college, including positions as athletic directors, coaches, officials, sportscasters, color commentators, authors of books, actors in films and advertisements, and leaders in business.

However, one thing that has eluded present-day players is a valid professional league where they could continue to play and support themselves financially. Hazel Walker, a five-time AAU All-American, organized the Arkansas Travelers, which played from 1949 until 1966, and one professional women's team, the All-American Red Heads, has been in existence since 1936. But while there have been many efforts to establish professional leagues in recent years, none of them have been successful. The first league attracting college athletes was established in 1978. It fell through in 1981, leaving many disillusioned athletes who had not been paid as promised.

Some American women began playing with professional basketball teams in Europe that year. Until there is sufficient support for women's professional basketball in the United States, the place to go after college may not be into professional leagues, but into the AAU program.

In the past decade of NCAA women's basketball, there have been many fine teams and coaches. Some of the teams posting wins most consistently have been Louisiana Tech, Texas, Long Beach State, Tennessee, Rutgers, Ohio State, N.C. State, Old Dominion, Mississippi, and Auburn.

Leon Barmore of Louisiana Tech and Pat Head Summitt of the University of Tennessee were voted Co-Coaches of the Decade (1980s) by the United States Basketball Writers Association. Between them, Barmore and Summitt had won five NCAA Championships; three of those were consecutive (Louisiana Tech won in 1988 and UT in 1987 and 1989). Pat Summitt took her third title at the 1991 NCAA Tournament in New Orleans.

Kay Yow of N.C. State coached the U.S. team to a gold medal in the 1979 World University Games, beat the Soviets twice in 1986 (at the Goodwill Games and the World Championship in Moscow), and guided the U.S. team to the gold medal in the 1988 Olympics in Seoul.

The nineties may well be the most exciting and fun-filled times for women's basketball. Many changes are taking place on college campuses, with continuing emphasis on the academic accomplishments of athletes, as witnessed by Pat Head Summitt, who during 17 years at the University of Tennessee has seen every four-year player graduate.

Her team drew 24,563 fans when they played Texas in 1987, and even though they were not in the finals of the 1990 NCAA Tournament in Knoxville, 16,595 fans showed up for the championship game (17,601 came for the semifinals). The fact that 34,196 spectators will come to watch women's basketball in two nights highlights the attraction of women's basketball in the nineties.

You will see some of the same excitement and intensity in this book. As you look at the photographs, imagine yourself there. Take time to glory in these marvelous athletes. Become one with the emotions that walk a tightrope between failure and success—between being a loser and a winner. Take in the wonder of it all as we celebrate a century of women's basketball.

Patsy Neal

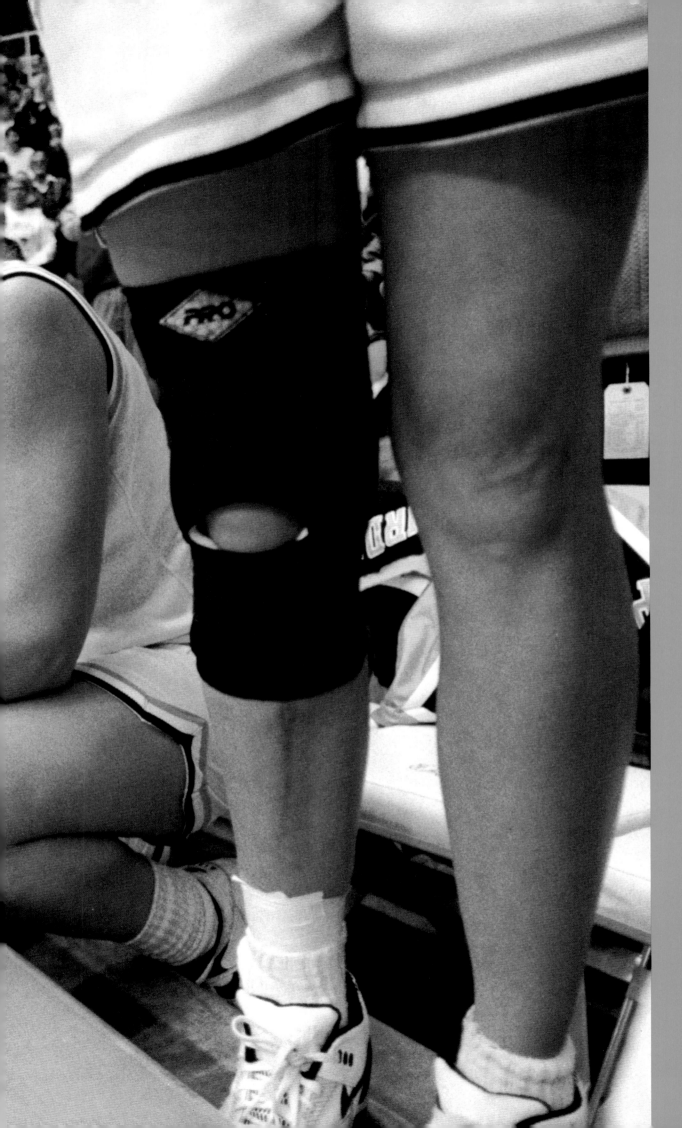

Purdue forward
Jane Calhoun cheers
teammates from the
bench in a home
game against Iowa.
Pauline Lubens

(Overleaf) At half
time during a game
with Louisiana State
University, Melissa
Peay passes the drill
team on her way to
the Stephen F. Austin
locker room.
Cindy Yamanaka

Hoping to win the spirit award handed out at the end of every home game, the Alpha Gamma Delta Sorority of Western Kentucky University cheers the Lady Toppers on against the University of Alabama.

Jeanie Adams

33

The Purdue team runs through a "tunnel of luck" formed by young fans in the Little Lady Boiler Club before a home game with Iowa.

The Maryland Terrapins walk on court for a workout before their game with Georgia in the Bell Atlantic Tournament in New Brunswick, New Jersey.

Maureen Holohan
of Northwestern,
forced to sit out the
year with a knee
injury, puts on a
brace before she goes
to a game against
Syracuse.

Mary Schroeder

Cindy Yamanaka

On the road for a game with Tennessee Tech, Michelle Thacker of Arkansas studies for a geology course in her hotel room.

Pat Greenhouse

Meri Simon

(*Above*) After a rigorous practice before a game with St. Anselm, Eileen Prendergast joins her Bentley College teammates to listen to her coach.

(*Left*) Tasha Bradley, a forward for UNLV, catches her breath on the bench during a game with Stanford.

Lois Bernstein

The demands of a hard practice show on the faces of Erina Queen (left), Jennifer Masters (center), and Hetti Dejong (right), as the University of Idaho players prepare for a game with Boise State in Moscow, Idaho.

Adrienne Helitzer

Christine Cotter

Jean Shifrin

(Above) UNLV cheer-
leaders and the team
warm up before a
home game with
Louisiana Tech.

(Left) A Clemson cheer-
leader concentrates on
balance and timing
during a home game
with Radford.

(Far left) A University of
Montana cheerleader
stirs up the fans for a
home game against
Montana State.

The Lady Cobbers of Concordia
College get psyched for the final
game of their Thanksgiving tournament in Moorhead, Minnesota.

Cindy Yamanaka

Arkansas forward Michelle Thacker reads a program while guard Sallie Moore (left) and forward Angie Gore (right) finish dressing for a game with Texas.

Pauline Lubens

Vying for space at a mirror, these Purdue teammates get ready for the real competition with the University of Iowa on Purdue's home court.

Pauline Lubens

Unlike many, these Purdue fans
are not content to be just faces
in the crowd.

Callie Shell

These Tennessee Tech ball girls pass
out basketballs and round them up
during pregame practice; during the
game they towel sweat off the floor
when players fall.

The Lady Longhorns of Texas
gather around coach Jody
Conradt during practice before
a game with Arkansas in
Fayetteville.

Pam Spaulding

Tennessee's Kelli Casteel has her
ankles taped in her hotel room
before a game with Louisiana Tech.

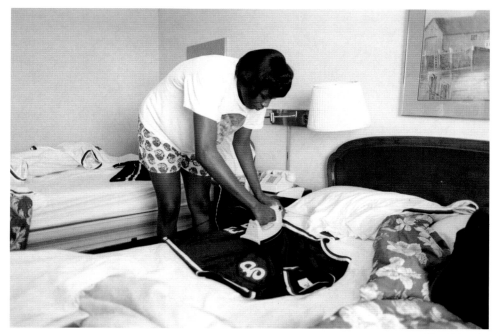

Mary Schroeder

Cindy Yamanaka

(Top) Stacey Ford irons her
Georgia uniform in a hotel
room before a game in the
SEC/Big Ten Challenge in
Albany, Georgia.

(Above) LSU guard Dana
Chatman studies in her
hotel room before a game
with Stephen F. Austin in
Nacogdoches, Texas.

Girl Scouts form the color guard for the national anthem during the Bell Atlantic Tournament.

Nicole Bengiveno

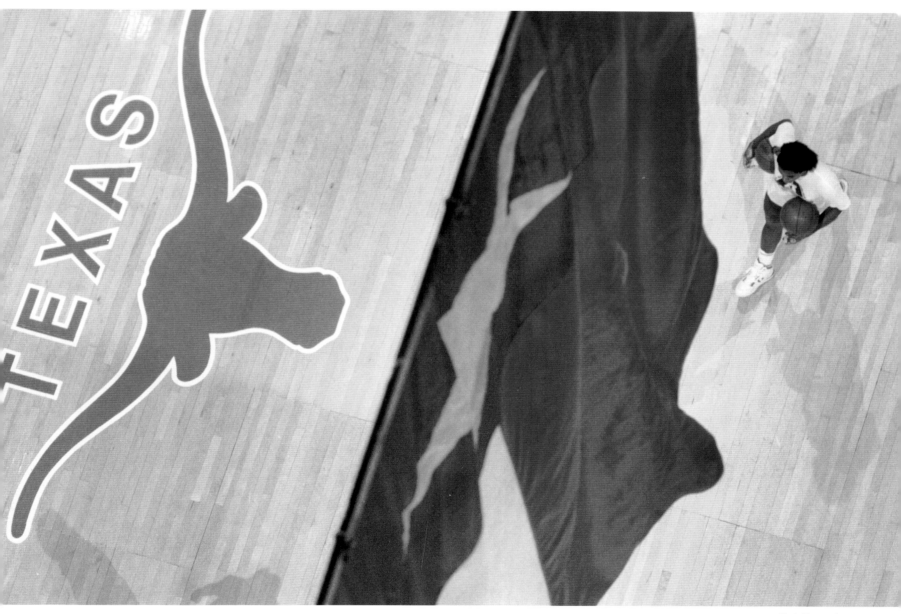

Cindy Yamanaka

Texas forward Joanne Benton leaves the court after practice the day of a home game with Arkansas.

(Left) Stanford assistant coach Julie Plank reviews strategy with her players before a home game with the University of Washington.

(Below) In preparation for an upcoming game with Texas, Arkansas head coach John Sutherland studies a video of their last contest.

Meri Simon

Cindy Yamanaka

(Facing) Steeped in basketball from the day he was born, Tyler Summitt rests on his mother's shoulder while she writes down a few points to hammer home to the Tennessee team before tip-off in the Super Shootout.

KEYS:
(1) TAKE CARE OF BALL
(2) DEFENSE
BALL PRESSURE
HELPSIDE
(3) BOARDS
BOX
+10

Pam Spaulding

(*Right*) Waiting their turn for warm-ups, the Lady Techsters observe the Stephen F. Austin team on the court.

(*Below*) Stanford guard Sonja Henning twirls a ball during practice at the Super Shootout in Hilton Head.

Susan Biddle

Callie Shell

During a time-out
in their game with
Luther College,
players from Concordia
huddle with head
coach Duane Siverson.

Players for Luther and Concordia position themselves under the ball in hopes of gaining possession during the Concordia Thanksgiving tournament.

Judy Griesedieck

Pauline Lubens

(Right) An Oklahoma State Cowgirl fan named Katie watches a home game against the University of Missouri with her father, Gary Boever.

(Facing) Members of the Little Lady Boiler Club have their own cheering section at Purdue's home games, this one played against Iowa.

Paula Nelson

Meri Simon

(Above) California band member Chris Hack beats the drum for his team during the Golden Bear Classic.

(Right) The last two St. Anselm players out of the locker room, Kimberly Mehlem (left) and Rachel Nyberg, sprint into the Bentley gym before game time.

Pat Greenhouse

Cindy Yamanaka

Jean Shifrin

(Top) On the way to a game with Stephen F. Austin, Louisiana State University team members alternately study and socialize.

(Above) Clemson players have their pregame meals in the "Tiger Den," a room set aside for them at a local restaurant. Courtney Johnson eats with two friends before leaving for a game with Radford.

Arkansas coach John Sutherland shares a lighthearted moment and a show of solidarity with the Lady Razorbacks on their home court.

Cindy Yamanaka

Cindy Yamanaka

Edna Campbell, guard for
the Texas Lady Longhorns,
exchanges "hook 'em horns"
signs with Ashley Davis before a
game with Arkansas in Austin.

Paula Nelson

In preparation for a home game with Tennessee, the Lady Longhorns warm up with stretches before their shoot-around.

Four Georgia players run back
to their hotel rooms just in time
to prepare for their SEC/Big Ten
Challenge game with Iowa.

(Facing) A speed dribble down-
court enables Georgia's Lady
Hardmon to break away from
Iowa in this SEC/Big Ten Challenge game.

Nicole Bengiveno

As a player on their team makes a
free throw in the Bell Atlantic Tournament, these Rutgers fans bring
their arms down and say "swoosh!"

Judy Griesedieck

Northern Illinois University fans
wave their arms while one of
their players takes a free throw.

(Left) Players race down-court in a game between Montana State and the University of Montana.

(Below) Sarah Flock of Montana State warms up before the game.

Christine Cotter

Christine Cotter

Paula Nelson

(*Above*) Guards Liz Brown and Paula Breeden of Oklahoma State work "low fives" into their free-throw drills before a game with the University of Missouri.

(*Right*) Athletes in their own right, cheerleaders for Stephen F. Austin State University stretch while the Ladyjacks begin their warm-up exercises in preparation for a home game against Louisiana State University.

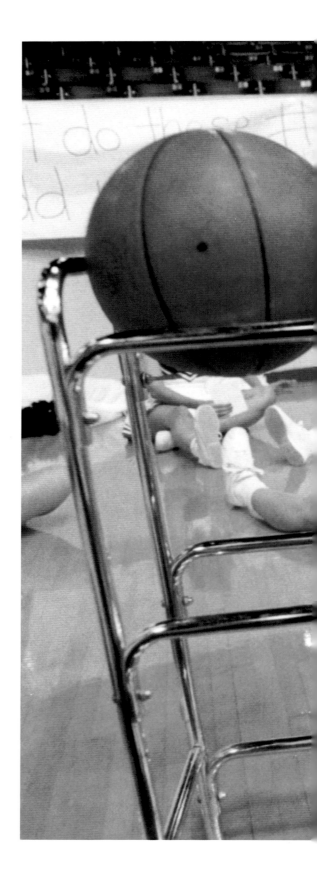

Pam Spaulding

The ref calls a blocking foul on an Ohio State player during a game with Texas in the Super Shootout.

Pam Spaulding

Texas forward Cinietra Henderson takes a free throw in a game against Ohio State during the Super Shootout in Hilton Head.

Arizona's Cheryl
Humphrey pressures
Terri Meyer of
Louisiana Tech in
the St. Joseph's
Tournament.

Vicki Valerio

University of California player Laura Baker brings the ball in while Clemson's Peggy Sells presses defense in the Golden Bear Classic at Berkeley.

Meri Simon

Amanda L. Alcock

A young girl roots
fiercely for her team in
a game between
Northern Illinois and
Vanderbilt.

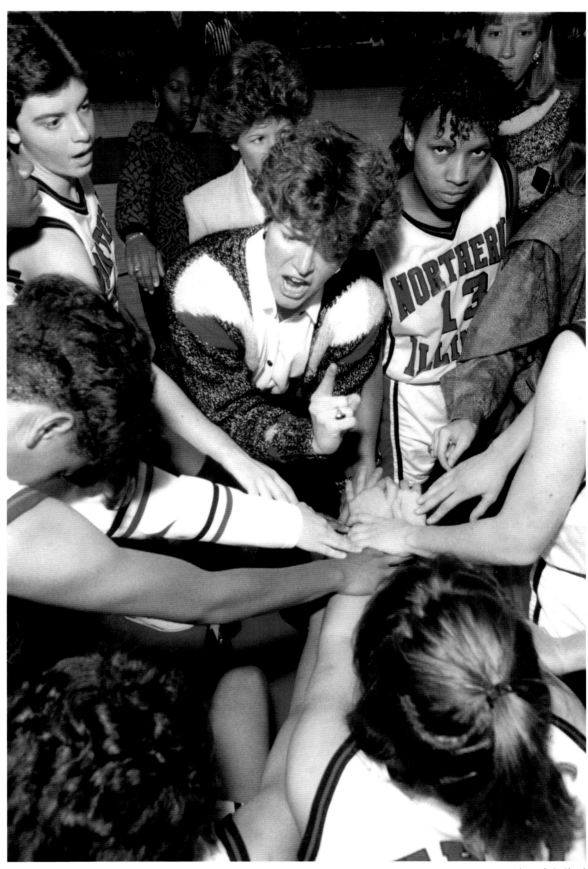

Northern Illinois head coach Jane Albright talks to her players in no uncertain terms before sending them back on the home court to play Vanderbilt.

Amanda L. Alcock

Marlene Karas

Action on the floor catches the attention of guard Danyel Parker and N.C. State head coach Kay Yow as they confer during the first half of a home game with the University of Virginia.

Looking for an open shot, Virginia forward Melanee Wagener instead gets Rhonda Mapp's hand in her face, while behind her, N.C. State's Sharon Manning provides a wall of defense.

Marlene Karas

Forward Jenny Kuziemski of N.C. State gives a yell as the ball is turned over to her team in triple overtime. Tonya Cardoza, who had just been called for traveling, slams the ball to the floor. Seconds later, Cardoza stole the ball to win the game for Virginia.

Kansas State's Mary
Jo Miller drives down-
court, closely guard-
ed by Oklahoma
State's Paula Breeden.

Mary Schroeder

Mary Schroeder

Liz Brown of Oklahoma State tries to press for the ball as Mary Jo Miller of Kansas State turns away in a game played in Manhattan, Kansas.

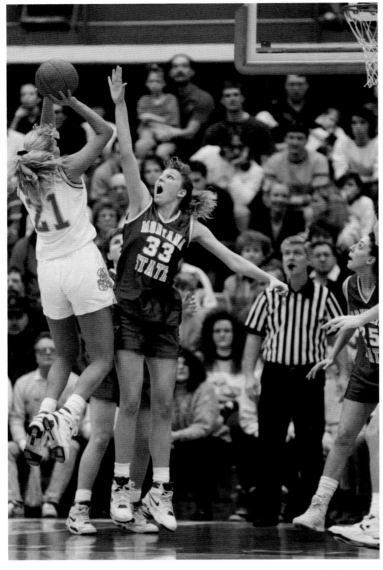

Christine Cotter

Montana State's
Denise Hockema
attempts to block a
jump shot from
Shannon Cate of
the University of
Montana.

During the Northern
Illinois Championship
in Dekalb, Iowa's
Nicole Tunsil drives
to the basket against
the University of
Michigan.

Judy Griesedieck

University of Washington forward Tara Davis comes in for a lay-up in a home game against UCLA.

Ellen M. Banner

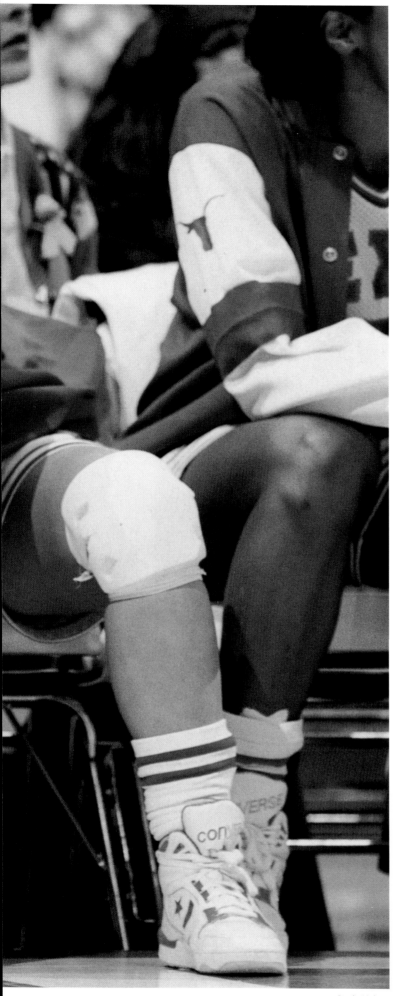

Paula Nelson

Mary Schroeder

Judy Griesedieck

(Top) Georgia players charge each other up as they are introduced before a SEC/Big Ten Challenge game with Iowa.

(Above) Northern Illinois head coach Jane Albright and her team enjoy a victory against Washington in the Northern Illinois Championship.

(Left) Texas teammates confer on the bench during a home game with Tennessee.

(Right) Heidi Klungel of Eastern Washington jumps to block as Angie Evans fakes and attempts a pass to a Boise State teammate.

(Facing) Mary Klemm of Arizona leaps in front of Louisiana Tech's Terri Meyer in hopes of distracting her during the St. Joseph's University Tournament.

Adrienne Helitzer

(Left) MaChelle Joseph of Purdue makes her own call for a charge as Iowa's Tonie Foster looks to the referee for his decision.

(Facing) There is no cheering in this corner, as the ref stops the clock and calls a foul on a Purdue player after she hits the floor during a game with Iowa.

Pauline Lubens

Pauline Lubens

Paula Nelson

Meri Simon

(Above) During half time at the Golden Bear Classic, fans shoot free throws in hopes of winning T-shirts and other prizes.

(Left) CBS broadcaster Mimi Griffin comments at half time during a game between Tennessee and Texas. This game, one of three aired on national TV during the regular season, was seen by a record 2.5 million people.

In pain from a separated shoulder, Meghan Pattyson of University of Connecticut gets help from the team doctor, Bruce Dick, during a game with Providence.

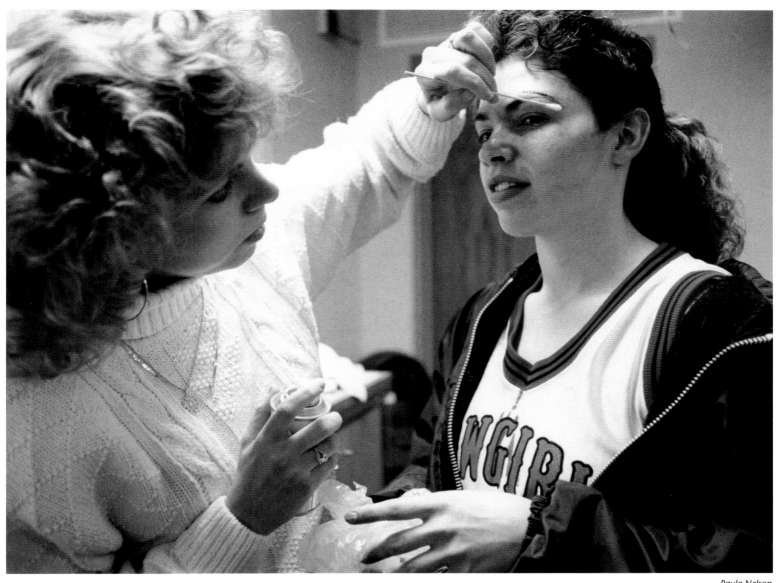

Mary Ellen Wolf, trainer for Oklahoma State University, applies antiseptic to 16 stitches above Liz Brown's eyebrow. The guard caught an elbow in the first half of a game with Missouri.

(Right) Grimacing in pain, Arizona's Timi Brown gets a hand up after a foul is called during a game with Louisana Tech in the St. Joseph's Tournament.

(Below) Sheila Ethridge of Louisiana Tech shoots over Arizona guard Mary Klemm, who appears to be taking off for a late jump.

Vicki Valerio

Vicki Valerio

Pam Spaulding

After winning against Louisiana
Tech, the Tennessee team winds
down in their locker room.

Callie Shell

After a home court loss to Stephen
F. Austin, Tennessee Tech players
Taunya Treanton, Dana Scott,
Angela Moorehead, and Rhea Beatty
mull over the game while waiting
for coach Bill Worrell's postmortem.

Christine Cotter

(Above) Forward Jodi Hinrichs of University of Montana follows through on a free throw as her teammates and Boise State players angle for position in the lane.

(Right) University of Iowa head coach Vivian Stringer (third from left) consults with her assistant coaches during practice at the Northern Illinois Championship.

Judy Griesedieck

Paula Bronstein

As Providence's Stephanie Cole goes
up for a shot, Meghan Pattyson of
Connecticut attempts to block her.

(Right) Daedra Charles pulls down a rebound for Tennessee under the Texas basket.

Paula Nelson

(Facing) Vicki Hall of Texas blocks out Tennessee's Daedra Charles for a rebound.

Paula Nelson

Mary Schroeder

Whatever these fans see at this
game between Northwestern and
Auburn in Evanston, it isn't anything
to jump up and down about.

Marlene Karas

(Above) University of South Carolina ball girl Jean Maron can hardly believe what she sees at the other end of the court in a game with the University of Georgia, while Hillary Dobson quietly takes it all in.

(Right) University of Washington band members watch the action on their home court in a game with UCLA.

Ellen M. Banner

(Above) Stanford's band plays on after a win against UNLV on Stanford's home court.

(Right) Stanford cheer-leader Ashanti Trent goes through her paces at a home game with UNLV.

(Facing) Notre Dame head coach Muffet McGraw talks with her team during time-out in a tournament game with St. Joseph's.

Vicki Valerio

Nicole Bengiveno

(Left) University of Maryland head coach Chris Weller urges the Terrapins on in a game against the University of Georgia in the Bell Atlantic Tournament.

(Below) Louisiana Tech head coach Leon Barmore has a word with guard Lisa Payne during a game with Tennessee.

(Right) Sue Gunter, head coach at LSU, talks with guard Dana Chatman during a game with Stephen F. Austin in Nacogdoches.

Pam Spaulding

Cindy Yamanaka

Mary Schroeder

(Above) Purdue's Joy Holmes and Auburn's Carolyn Jones scramble for a loose ball in their SEC/Big Ten Challenge game.

(Right) Marlene Ferguson of Michigan State gets a helping hand from a teammate during a game against Iowa in the Northern Illinois Championship.

(Facing) Elbows out, Washington's Tara Davis fights to get a little room after grabbing a rebound in a game against Stanford.

Judy Griesedieck

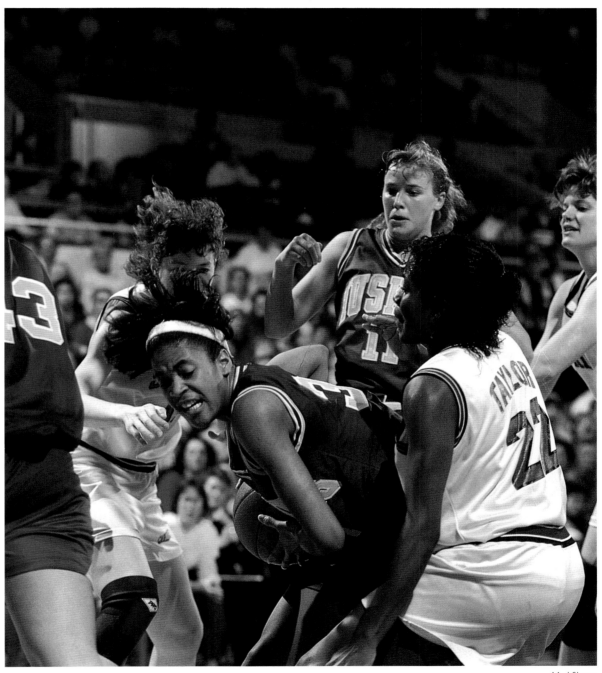

Meri Simon

(Left) Nebraska head coach Angela Beck points out a weakness in defense before sending in guard Kristi Dahn during the second half of a game with Kansas State.

(Below) Nebraska forward Rissa Taylor yells back to confirm her coach's instructions before running on court in the second half of a home game with Kansas State.

(Facing) Kansas State forward Jennifer Grebing defends as Sue Hesch attempts to score for Nebraska on her home court.

Mary E. Schulte

Mary E. Schulte

Lynn Stevenson (left) and Kim Mays of Auburn cheer their team in a game with Purdue in the SEC/Big Ten Challenge.

Mary Schroeder

University of Washington forward Erika Hardwick vents her frustration after fouling Lisa Foss of Northern Illinois.

Judy Griesedieck

In an intense moment
during a game with
Louisiana Tech, Muffet
McGraw tries to get a
time-out for Notre Dame.

Vicki Valerio

Meri Simon

With 30 seconds on the clock and a 67-67 score, fans from both Washington and Stanford hope that time is on their side.

Vicki Valerio

Vicki Valerio

(Above) A fan in the stands lets his pennant do the talking for him at an Army-Navy game in Annapolis.

(Left) Jubilant after their victory, Army players shake hands with Navy.

Pam Spaulding

Tennessee's Daedra
Charles laces up an ankle
support before a home
game against Stanford.

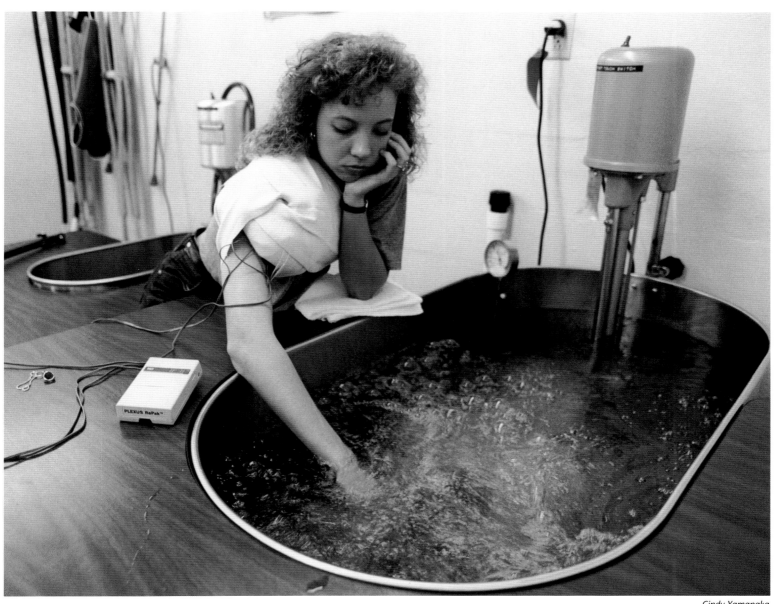

Cindy Yamanaka

Stacey Brown of Stephen F. Austin soothes her sprained thumb in a warm bath. Electrode therapy before and after games helps decrease the pain and muscle spasms in the guard's partially dislocated shoulder.

Judy Griesedieck

(Above) After winning their tournament, Northern Illinois players Angela Lockett, Cindy Conner, and Denise Dove autograph a fan's sweatshirt.

(Right) Twelve-year-old Tori Barker, who hopes to play collegiate basketball someday, gets an autograph from N.C. State forward Krissy Kuziemski after a home game with Maryland.

Jean Shifrin

Amanda L. Alcock

Proud of their team, two young boys show off their homemade signs during a Northern Illinois game with Vanderbilt.

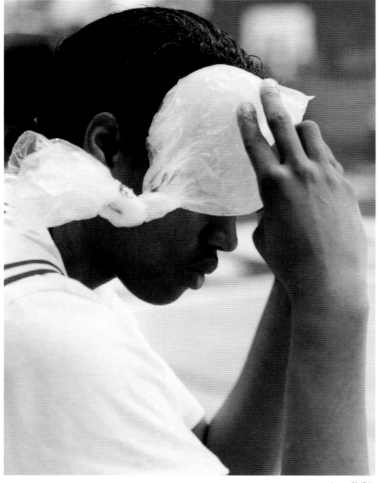

Jean Shifrin

(Above) Forward Sharon Manning of N.C. State holds ice against her forehead after she was elbowed during a home game with Maryland.

(Right) Texas forward Courtney Canavan stretches out with a heat pack on her back before a game with Tennessee.

Paula Nelson

Mary Schroeder

The Kansas State team whoops
it up after winning against
Oklahoma State in overtime.

Pam Spaulding

Coach Pat Summitt's young niece, Casey Attebery, joins the Tennessee team in their locker room after a win over Stanford at the Super Shootout.

Rebecca Barger

Kansas forward Misti Chennault rises to cheer her team in the final moments of a home game with Missouri.

(Facing) Taneshia Welch and Karen Zajick of Syracuse listen to their coach describe what they have to do to come from behind in the second half of a game with Northwestern.

Lois Bernstein

After losing to the University of Idaho by one point, Heather Cogswell of Idaho State takes time to compose herself in the locker room.

Paula Nelson

"Pistol Pete" looks concerned as the Oklahoma State Cowgirls struggle in competition against the Missouri Tigers.

Vicki Valerio

(Above) Notre Dame forward Comalita Haysbert has a moment to think about her next move during a game with St. Joseph's in the St. Joseph's Tournament.

(Left) Latonya Tate (center) of Iowa hugs teammate Andrea Harmon after winning a game against Purdue on Purdue's home court.

Pauline Lubens

Reneé Hannans

(Facing) Melissa Thomas of Mississippi State relaxes on the bench during a game with Mississippi in the SEC Tournament.

(Left) University of Kentucky cheerleaders prepare to catch their partners after a dismount during the SEC Tournament.

(Below) During the SEC Tournament, Heather Case of the University of Georgia pep band solos in an underground passage to the James Gray Civic Center in Albany, Georgia.

Reneé Hannans

Marlene Karas

Marlene Karas

LSU's Sheila Johnson dribbles out from under Georgia's Stacey Ford (right), while LSU's Dana Chatman (far left) tries to break away from Camille Lowe in their SEC Tournament semifinal game.

Marlene Karas

A score against Mississippi in the
SEC Tournament quarter finals gives
Auburn fan Richard Henderson
something to cheer about.

Marlene Karas

After winning the SEC Tournament Championship, joyful LSU teammates embrace, while the Tennessee team walks over to shake their hands.

Marlene Karas

LSU forward Barbara Henderson cuts down the net after her team won the SEC Championship game.

Paula Bronstein/Hartford Courant

(Left) Connecticut forward Kerry Bascom gets a word from her coach, Geno Auriemma, in the final moments of a game with Providence in the Big East Tournament.

(Facing) Off balance and on her way down with Syracuse guard Charie Crouse, Connecticut guard Debbie Baer tries to retain the ball.

Paula Bronstein/Hartford Courant

Lynn Johnson

(Above) An Oklahoma State player blocks out Lisa Sanbothe of Missouri, who is looking for a rebound during the Big Eight Tournament.

(Right) Exhausted after his antics in a game between Colorado and Oklahoma, Tony Burnham, the Colorado mascot, collapses in a stadium lounge.

Lynn Johnson

Lynn Johnson

Lynn Johnson

(Above) Misti Chennault of the University of Kansas challenges a Colorado player for possession of the ball in the Big Eight Tournament.

(Left) In the last few minutes of a game with Oklahoma State, Missouri coach Joann Rutherford realizes that her team will probably lose.

Donna Bagby

Tiffany Beard of Tuett-McConnell College guards Tonya McJimson from Hinds Community College in a play-off game in the National Junior College Athletic Association Women's Tournament hosted by Tyler Junior College in Tyler, Texas.

Donna Bagby

On the edge of their seats, Odessa College players watch their teammates fight to keep their lead in a close game with Northeastern Oklahoma.

(Left) A knee injury benches Cassandra Lumpkins of Central Arizona College during a play-off game with Hilbert College in the National Junior College Athletic Association Women's National Tournament.

(Above) Odessa players take turns cutting the net after defeating Northeastern Oklahoma A&M College to win the NJCAA Women's National Tournament.

Mary Schroeder

During half time in the ACC Championship game, Clemson coach Jim Davis tries to pump up his team and get them to focus on what they have to do to win.

Mary Schroeder

The final moments of Duke's
loss to Clemson in the ACC
Tournament are hard for the
Blue Devils to take sitting down.

Vicki Valerio

Virginia's Heidi Burge attempts a lay-up in the last seconds of the semifinal ACC game with Clemson, while her teammate Dawn Staley (far left) yells for a chance at a three-pointer.

Mary Schroeder

Clemson spirits run high after
the team edges out Virginia in
the ACC semifinals.

(Facing) Virginia's Tonya Cardoza goes up for a basket as LeAnn Kennedy of North Carolina tries to tip it out during the first round of the ACC Tournament in Fayetteville, North Carolina.

Vicki Valerio

(Right) Andrea Stinson of N.C. State cuts down the net after her team's win against Clemson made N.C. State the ACC Tournament champions.

Vicki Valerio

Vicki Valerio

Vicki Valerio

(Above) Penn State's head coach Rene Portland and forward Lynn Dougherty communicate with two different players on the court during the Atlantic Ten Conference semifinal game with West Virginia.

(Right) Forward Wendy Brink of St. Joseph's University doubles over in pain after a fall in the Atlantic Ten Conference Championship game with Penn State.

(Left) Penn State's Lynn Dougherty celebrates with her team after winning the Atlantic Ten Conference Championship on their home court.

Vicki Valerio

Lisa Waddell-Buser

Nelson C. Brownlee, head coach of
Claflin College, talks with Felicia Boyles
during a game with Fort Hays State
University in the National Association of
Intercollegiate Athletics Tournament in
Jackson, Tennessee. Fort Hays went on
to win the championship in the final
game against Southwestern.

Lisa Waddell-Buser

Southwestern Oklahoma State University played Indiana University-Purdue University in the NAIA Tournament. During half time, Southwestern players rest in the locker room and listen to their coach.

Pam Spaulding

(Left) Daedra Charles of Tennessee and Stanford's Val Whiting go for a loose ball in the semifinals of the Women's Final Four in New Orleans.

(Below) Though the color cardinal is the only officially recognized symbol of Stanford's athletic teams, unofficial mascots have come and gone. This one, called "The Tree," seems to poke fun at the whole idea.

(Facing) After her team's loss to Tennessee in the semifinal game, a Stanford player takes a moment to grieve.

Mary Schroeder

159

160

(Facing) Virginia guard Tammi Reiss pressures Laura Lishness of Connecticut during the semifinals of the Women's Final Four in New Orleans.

(Right) Virginia guard Dawn Staley calls the next play in the semifinal game with Connecticut.

(Below) Double-teamed by Connecticut players Wendy Davis (left) and Debbie Baer (right), Dena Evans of Virginia brings the ball upcourt in the Women's Final Four semifinals.

Mary Schroeder

Mary Schroeder

Pam Spaulding

(Facing) Virginia's Heather Burge and Daedra Charles of Tennessee tip-off at the opening of the Women's Final Four Championship game.

(Right) Daedra Charles tries to block Tonya Cardoza's shot as the Virginia forward goes up for a basket.

(Below) Peggy Evans lunges to save the ball for Tennessee as it goes out-of-bounds.

Pam Spaulding

Pam Spaulding

(Above) Tonya Cardoza consoles her Virginia teammate Dawn Staley after she fouls out in overtime.

(Left) Peggy Evans and her teammates revel in the 70-67 victory over Virginia which brought Tennessee its third NCAA Women's Basketball Championship in five years.

Dana Fineman

A **NATIVE OF** Paramus, New Jersey, Maria DeVita played forward for Georgetown University when she was a premed student. Her schedule was hectic—classes from eight to five, basketball practice from seven thirty to nine thirty, and a lot of study time in between.

"Practice gave me an outlet and helped clear my head," she says. "Having to organize my schedule so that I could both study and play taught me to concentrate and set priorities." These are skills she now finds invaluable in her still busy life as a doctor, wife, and mother.

After graduating from medical school in 1984 and completing her internship and residency, she decided to subspecialize in kidney diseases because she felt the continued training would make her a better internist. Today DeVita has a private practice and also teaches and conducts research at Lenox Hill Hospital in New York, where she serves as assistant chief of nephrology. She is married to Keith Meyers, who is Associate Athletic Director at Seton Hall University.

DeVita held the Hoya record for career rebounds for almost a decade, despite the fact that she only played with the team for three years. Not only could she anticipate how the shots would fall from either side of the basket, but at 5'8", she could also touch the rim. She says she hopes her children inherit her jumping abilities, not her shooting skills.

She still finds the time to play basketball with a group that includes the coach of her rival high school team. The mother of an infant daughter named Emma, DeVita will encourage her child to be active in sports, if not to compete, then for fitness. "There's still an attitude in society that it's okay for women to work out," she says, "but to become an athlete . . . girls are still much more likely to say they want to be actresses than athletes. That's a bit disconcerting.

"Though women's programs are far behind the men's in some ways, we have the opportunity to make sports a better learning experience," she says. "If sports are integrated into life, they can make you more ready for life."

Dana Fineman

WHEN THE OWNER of the Indiana Pacers called Ann Meyers in 1979 and invited her to try out, the former UCLA star thought it was a joke. At 24 the oldest player on the U.S. National Team, she felt she was being phased out of play. And now, Sam Nassi was offering her a chance that most men never have, to play in the NBA.

Despite the skepticism of many, including her brother David, who was playing for the Milwaukee Bucks, Meyers took the offer and tried out. She didn't make the team, but her work as color commentator for twelve Pacers games that season has led to a career in broadcasting that includes coverage of men's and women's sports on radio, ESPN, and network television.

"People keep saying that attitudes about women playing competitive sports with men will change in five to ten years, but they've been saying that for the last fifty years," she says. Even so, Meyers has done her share to move things along for the women's game.

A graduate of Sonora High School in La Habra, California, she was the first high school player to be selected for the U.S. National Team and the first woman to receive a full athletic scholarship to UCLA. In 1976, the year women's basketball was first included in the Olympics, Meyers helped her team win the silver medal in Montreal.

Meyers averaged 17.4 points and 8.4 rebounds per game at UCLA and still holds the school record for career assists. She helped lead her team to the AIAW National Collegiate Women's Basketball Championship in 1978. That same year she was awarded the Broderick Cup as the outstanding female athlete and was named the College Women's Basketball Player of the Year. She was the first four-time Kodak All-American, male or female. In 1979, she was the first woman to carry the U.S. flag in the Pan Am Games.

The mother of two, Meyers continues her work as a color commentator in a field she considers every bit as competitive as the sport itself. It was through broadcasting that she met her husband, baseball Hall of Famer and fellow sports commentator Don Drysdale, when she competed in the Superstars.

Dana Fineman

A **KODAK ALL-AMERICAN** point guard for Immaculata College, Marianne Stanley stayed on as a part-time coaching assistant in women's basketball after graduating in 1976. A year later, she was hired as head coach at Old Dominion, where she compiled a 269-59 record over a decade. Her team won the NIT title in her first season, AIAW titles in 1979 and 1980, and the NCAA crown in 1985. As a player and a coach, she has been to the Women's Final Four ten times.

"In team sports," says Stanley, "one of the greatest challenges is to pull a group together so that everyone knows their contribution is important." In this light, she considers her experience as assistant coach with the U.S. team at the 1986 World Championship in Moscow one of the best in her notable career. She credits head coach Kay Yow for establishing a collegial atmosphere from the start. "Each player had been the best on her team," says Stanley. "For some, it was the first time that being outstanding wouldn't necessarily mean that they would play a lot. Sometimes a person's darker side comes out. But those kids were great. When we won the gold medal, the Soviets were dumbstruck."

Stanley left Old Dominion for the University of Pennsylvania in 1987; in two years, she compiled an 11-41 record. "At Penn, a nonscholarship school, I couldn't recruit the best athletes," she says. "I realized that one of my main motivations is having a chance to go to the dance and win it all."

In 1989, she was hired as head coach at the University of Southern California, where the athletic program allows her to join in fierce competition for the best players. "Recruiting takes a tremendous amount of time and energy," says Stanley. "Think about the coach who finished second, who didn't get the recruit. You get it all, or you get nothing."

As the mother of 16-year-old Michelle, she is also especially concerned about providing today's young women with role models. "From grade school through college, I was coached by women," says Stanley. "In the 1970s, 70 percent of the head coaches for women's basketball were women. Now it's about 40 percent. After Title IX, we had more opportunities and better salaries in women's basketball, and men started competing for the jobs. Sometimes it seems women coaches are becoming an endangered species."

Dana Fineman

LYNETTE WOODARD is the NCAA's all-time leading scorer in women's basketball: with 3,649 points, she is second only to Pete Maravich. She began honing her skills at the age of eight in a game she and her brother called "sockball" and played by shooting a rolled pair of their father's dress socks over the bedroom closet and entry doors. They faked dribbles, but their lay-ups, dunks, hooks, and jumpers were real. "When my mother realized we were trying to play basketball," says Woodard, "she bought us a hoop and ball."

Recruited by the University of Kansas in 1978, Woodard helped lead the Jayhawks to a 108-32 record in her four years. She won the Broderick Cup and the Wade Trophy in 1981, and was named the Big Eight Conference Player of the Decade. A four-time Kodak All-American and a two-time Academic All-American, she graduated in 1981 with a B.A. in communications. Woodard made the Olympic teams in 1980 and 1984, and was the captain of the gold medal-winning team in Los Angeles in 1984.

In 1985, she became the first woman to play with the Harlem Globetrotters. The fulfillment of a long-time dream, it was also more fun than she had imag-

ined. "Playing with those guys is like changing the dial from R and B to jazz," says Woodard, who was with the team for two years. "I refined my skills and worked a different part of the game to perfection."

A veteran of professional basketball in Italy, she describes the European game as fast and very physical. She is more comfortable playing in Japan, where the style is faster but not as rough. "I like their game because I love to run. The Japanese take pride in their outside shooting—30-footers go up with incredible accuracy. I love their attitude and their kind of practice. In the States, practices are usually two hours; in Japan they are four. No matter how they feel, everyone comes to play.

"Until we pay women what they deserve," says Woodard, "they won't be able to play professional basketball in the U.S. It's all about economics. If we paid women $150,000 to $200,000 a year, which is nothing compared with the million dollars Magic Johnson earns, you would see exciting women's basketball in this country, and you would enjoy it." For now, though, Lynette Woodard will continue to play in Japan.

Barbara M. Trammell

SHOOTING HOOPS as a young girl in Dubach, Louisiana, Mary Currie set her sights on earning a basketball scholarship. In her constant search to improve her game, she regularly played boys who were five to ten years older. She also competed with her brothers and sisters, one on three, and attended summer basketball camp.

In seventh grade, she joined the junior varsity team; in eighth, she made varsity at Dubach High School. By the time Currie was offered scholarships in her senior year, she had researched job markets and decided that the computer field would afford her the best opportunities and the highest pay for an entry-level position.

She chose to attend Grambling State University because it offered a good computer science program close to home. As in high school, Currie was the leading scorer on her team. Most of her shots were taken close in; she went to the free-throw line an average of ten to twelve times each game. "Most of the time," says Currie, "shooting that close to the bucket, I really had to work at keeping the defense moving and getting free."

Currie enjoyed the attention she received as one of the outstanding players on her team. "Basketball did a lot for my confidence and my self-esteem," she says. "It also helped my attitude. Being part of a team helped me open up so that I became more sensitive to other people. The discipline and the pressure to perform helped me prepare for the business world."

Graduating with a B.S. in computer science in 1987, she joined General Dynamics as a software engineer. She now works for Unisys Corporation in the same capacity, while earning her M.B.A. at the University of Houston. Some day she would like to own her own business or manage a computer data center.

Currie stays in shape by jogging four days a week and lifting weights. For recreation and relaxation, she plays tennis with her friends and colleagues. "I don't play basketball anymore," she says, "There's so much running—and it's too intense."

Barbara M. Trammell

WHEN **MIMI GRIFFIN** talks about women's basketball, she draws upon a rich family heritage. Her grandmother and her mother both played in the Philadelphia Catholic leagues, and when Griffin made the varsity basketball team at Lancaster Catholic High School in 1970, she asked for the same number her sister Barbara had worn four years before. Wearing that number, she scored 44 points one night to break her sister's single-game record. "In my mind," says Griffin, who was MVP in the state championship her senior year, "when they retired my uniform, they also retired my sister's."

She continued to play basketball at the University of Pittsburgh, though she describes that as a letdown after her storybook years in high school. Graduating in 1978 with a B.A. in economics, she earned a masters in business administration from Lehigh University in 1979. She was project director for special events for Manufacturers Hanover Trust and director of national promotions in women's athletics for Converse before starting her own company, MSG Promotions, which specializes in the management and promotion of special events.

Since 1983, Griffin has worked with CBS, ESPN, and the NCAA as a color analyst for women's basketball games. In 1990, she became the first woman to broadcast on-the-air analysis of a men's NCAA basketball tournament game, Notre Dame versus Virginia. She has a reputation for meticulous pregame research that includes watching tapes and practices and making detailed charts of statistics and interesting personal facts about the players on each team. "I probably overprepare by about 70 percent," says Griffin. "Only then do I feel comfortable on the air." She credits her high school coach with teaching her the "whys" of the game as well as how to play, something that pays off in her careful analysis of games for TV viewers. Once her biggest thrill was running a fastbreak with her teammates, but now she is most impressed with the fundamentals. "The things that don't show up on stat sheets," she says, "are the things that drive me wild."

In addition to her work in broadcasting, Griffin is tournament director for the 1992 Seniors Open Golf Tournament at the Saucon Valley Country Club in Pennsylvania. She lives in Allentown with her husband Bill Griffin, a former basketball player at Lehigh University, and their four-year-old son Kyle.

Dana Fineman

I N 1977, a crowd of 10,000 people watched Montclair State play Queens in Madison Square Garden, a game Carol Blazejowski will never forget. The junior forward scored 52 points for Montclair, setting a single-game record for the Garden that held for both women and men for a decade, and Blazejowski's team came from behind in the second half to win. She recalls, "Everything came together: one of my finest shooting games, a great crowd, and a victory in the mecca of basketball."

From an early age, "Blaze" has worked at shooting accurately inside and outside from both sides of the basket. She is a tireless student of the sport. "I would take, borrow, and steal a little bit of everybody's game," she says. "If I saw a move I liked, I'd take it down to the court and work on it."

In her senior year, little-known Montclair State made it to the Final Four, a "mission accomplished" for Blazejowski and her teammates, who sorely wanted the recognition for their nonscholarship school. For Blazejowski, it was a dramatic way to wind up her four years at Montclair, where she averaged 31.7 points per game, earned a 38.6 scoring

average in her senior year, and had a career total of 3,199. She graduated with a B.S. in physical education in 1978, holding nearly every offensive and defensive record at Montclair.

A three-time Kodak All-American and the winner of the first Wade Trophy, Blazejowski was a silver medalist in the 1979 Pan American Games and a gold medalist in the World Championship Games. She was also selected for the 1980 Olympic team. In 1981, she was the MVP and the professional league's leading scorer with the New Jersey Gems.

Today, she is the director of licensing for the NBA, working with manufacturers to develop new products which incorporate team logos and players' likenesses. She plays basketball four times a week and leads a barnstorming AAU team that challenges college teams before the regular season.

Outspoken in her convictions, Blazejowski believes that women athletes have a responsibility to be positive role models and to get involved in furthering the public's perception of women's sports. "After I'm gone," she tells her kids in basketball camp, "you'll be the ones to carry on."

Dana Fineman

HOLLY **WARLICK** played basketball at Knoxville's Bearden High School in the days of six-on-six. It was a slower game than she might have liked, but she remembers the adjustment to five-on-five at the University of Tennessee as difficult. "At first, I was a hyper player, with no control over my speed or my talent. I shot one for eight in my first game. All the shots I missed were lay-ups, thrown with such speed and force that they practically banked back to half-court. I probably gave my coach a couple of gray hairs."

Limiting her shooting opportunities, coach Pat Summitt challenged Warlick to be a good defensive player. "She saw my strengths and took advantage of them, and I was willing to accept the role she chose for me. Everything she told me to do, I did."
Summitt's strategy and Warlick's hard work and dedication proved a successful combination. As point guard, she became known for relentless defense and for her contribution to the fastbreak.

From 1976 to 1980, Warlick was awarded All-State, All-Region, All-Conference, and Kodak All-American honors and led the Lady Vols to the AIAW Championship games three times. She broke the

school's records for assists and steals, and became the first player in the 95-year history of athletics at Tennessee to have her jersey retired.

In 1977, she was on the U.S. Junior National team: the following year she played on the National team. In 1979, her teams won a gold medal in the World Championship and the Jones Cup, and a silver medal at the Pan American Games. She made the 1980 Olympic team, but her hopes were dashed with the U.S. boycott. "I was so bitter," she recalls, "I couldn't watch the 1984 Olympics, even though Pat Summitt was the coach."

Warlick played professionally with the Nebraska Wranglers, helping them win the World Championship in 1981. After the team folded, she completed her marketing degree at UT. From 1981 to 1983, she was assistant coach at Virginia Tech, where she also earned her masters in athletic administration. She gained two years of experience as assistant coach at the University of Nebraska before returning to Tennessee in 1986. As assistant coach under Pat Summitt, she has helped lead the Lady Vols to the Women's Final Four five times in the past six seasons.

Barbara M. Trammell

DEDICATION, Determination, Desire. Through athletics, the three Ds were instilled in Beth Bass from the age of twelve. "I was in a highly structured situation in which I learned to believe in myself," she says, and throughout her professional life, she has worked to support the kind of positive athletic experience she herself has had.

As a forward playing for Pat Hewitt at Hartsville High School in South Carolina, Bass was an All-Conference selection three times, an All-State honoree twice, and the second all-time leading scorer in her high school's history.

In her senior year at Hartsville, Bass was offered a basketball scholarship at East Tennessee State University, where she played guard. In 1981, her sophomore year, she injured her knee during practice. She spent 11 months on crutches and played between four surgeries. "Though it was frustrating, I can still say that those were the best years of my life. The bonding and the energy I felt being part of a collegiate team were tremendous."

Bass graduated cum laude in 1984 with a double major in public relations and political science. In the same year, she was hired as a graduate assistant in sports information, promotions, and marketing with the University of Tennessee athletic department. "I had an opportunity to get in on the ground level of promotions for women's sports with one of the strongest athletic programs for women in the country," says Bass. In 1986, she received her masters in recreation administration.

In her current position with Converse as national promotions manager, Bass has found an ideal outlet for her energy and enthusiasm for women's sports, as she travels across the country to manage special events, give talks at basketball camps and clinics, and work with collegiate accounts. She also coordinates strategies for national marketing and promotional opportunities in women's athletics, working closely with the Women's Basketball Coaches Association and the Women's Final Four.

Sgt. Heidi Daugherty, U.S. Army

ON OCTOBER 28, 1990, Army First Lieutenant Stacey Cagenello arrived in Saudi Arabia to serve with a transportation battalion in Operation Desert Shield. As Battalion Adjutant, the 26-year-old officer supervised all personnel functions for more than 900 service men and women in a unit charged with hauling food, water, ammunition, and spare parts by truck convoy to the front lines. At war's end, the unit began backhauling supplies through the desert and processing them for departure; responsible for getting everyone else out first, the group was among the last to return to the United States.

Cagenello considers taking part in the desert operation a high point in her military and civilian life. "It's been a good learning experience—not just participating in the military, but having to adapt to another culture," she says. "My experience in the Army has given me leadership responsibilities and excellent management skills. At 22, my first job was to manage 40 people I didn't know."

She joined the Army following ROTC training at Lafayette College in Pennsylvania, where she gradu-

ated in 1987 with a B.A. in economics. Cagenello played guard on Lafayette's basketball team, scoring 1,521 points and leading her team to two conference championships.

The 5'8" guard has continued to develop her game while playing for the All-Army and the Armed Forces teams. In 1988, she was named AAU Rookie of the Year; the following year, her Armed Forces team placed third in the AAU National Championship. In 1990, she was named both Armed Forces Female Athlete of the Year and Army Female Athlete of the Year. Playing basketball in the Armed Forces took a little getting used to. "In the Army," she says, "we play a much faster, more physical game with less discipline. It's survival of the fittest, just run and gun."

Interested in sports from her early years in Harwinton, Connecticut, Cagenello credits her family for their open-mindedness concerning athletics. "Though my parents were never athletes," she says, "they have always supported me along the way." In the fall of 1991, Cagenello will become head coach at West Point Prep School in Monmouth, New Jersey.

Dana Fineman

"**B**ASKETBALL gave me an education at one of the best universities, the opportunity to live in Europe, and the job of my dreams," says Val Ackerman, who serves as special assistant to National Basketball Association Commissioner David Stern. She also reviews players' contracts, helps facilitate trades, and works on issues related to the Olympics, now that professional players will be allowed to compete.

"My connections with basketball are lifelong in every sense," says Ackerman, whose father and grandfather were players and coaches. She was one of Debbie Ryan's first scholarship players at the University of Virginia, and her first year at UVA was Ryan's first year as head coach.

"Debbie and I are from the same town and high school. That was one reason I came to Virginia. She has always been very committed to coaching and to her team. Six weeks before the beginning of practice, I was running the cross-country trails, training with weights, and handling the ball. We were expected to stay in training in the off-season and join a summer league." Though the program was rigorous, her team only won 9 out of 26 games her freshman year. By her senior year, the vastly improved Cavaliers were 22 and 10 and nationally ranked.

After graduating with high honors in political and social thought, Ackerman played basketball with a semiprofessional team in Cosné sur Loire, France. The only American on a team she considered mediocre, and frustrated by the delay in getting her eligibility papers, she returned to the U.S. and entered law school at UCLA. After graduation in 1985, Ackerman worked with a Wall Street law firm. In 1988, she was able to connect basketball with her legal career by becoming staff attorney for the National Basketball Association, an assignment which lead to her present position with the commissioner. Ackerman lives in Manhattan with her husband, Charles Rappaport.

Dana Fineman

FROM THE TIME she was featured in her first newspaper article at the age of 13, Cheryl Miller has been something of a media phenomenon. While playing for Riverside Poly High School, she became the first woman ever to dunk in a regulation game. She scored 105 points in another. Camera crews followed her to school. "I loved all the attention," says Miller, whose parents intervened whenever things got overwhelming for her. "The more I received, the harder I worked. Just when people thought they knew me and how I could play, I would surprise them and do something different."

Miller became the most sought-after recruit in the history of women's sports. In her senior year, the floor of her room was covered with stacks of letters sent by more than 250 schools offering her scholarships. When she made up her mind to go to the University of Southern California, she called a press conference to announce her decision.

In four years at USC, Miller claimed nearly every school record. She totaled 3,018 points, 1,534 rebounds, 1,159 field goals, and 702 free throws. She led USC to a 112-20 record; in her four years they made it to the Women's Final Four three times and

won two national championships. A four-time Kodak All-American and a three-time Naismith Award winner, Miller also received the Broderick Cup in 1984 and the Wade Trophy in 1985. She was a gold medal winner in the 1984 Olympics in Los Angeles. In 1986, she graduated from USC with a degree in sports information.

Miller is currently a commentator for ABC Sports, covering the sidelines for college football and both color and sidelines for men's collegiate basketball. "Being a color commentator for basketball is the greatest job in the world," she laughs, "because now I can criticize coaches and officials without getting thrown out of the game."

She would also like to announce amateur boxing matches and prize fights. "I've always been a big boxing fan," says Miller, "maybe because it's the most selfish sport. You can't rely on anyone else, you can't blame anyone. It comes down to whether you had the desire and commitment to get yourself into the best shape emotionally and physically for that fight." To enhance her effectiveness on the air, Miller is currently taking acting lessons.

Dana Fineman

WHEN FBI SPECIAL agent Tiphanie Bates knocks on a fugitive's door, she never knows what to expect. But her pounding heart and the kick of adrenaline are signs of a kind of stress she actually enjoys. After 17 weeks of training at the academy in Quantico, Virginia, she is confident that she can handle most situations. "People are driven by different challenges," she says. "I'm always looking for excitement."

Bates works out some of the pressure of her job by playing basketball with her fellow agents. Most are men, but she holds her own in their company—she played point guard for Whitesburg High School in Whitesburg, Kentucky, from 1979 to 1983, and for Morehead State University, where she graduated in 1987. After she earned a law degree from the University of Kentucky in 1990, she applied to the FBI. "By the middle of my second year of law school," she recalls, "I knew I wouldn't enjoy practicing law. I don't want to sit behind a desk—I've got to be moving around."

Her coach at MSU, Loretta Marlow, remembers the 5'6" guard as a dedicated player and intense competitor, both traits which serve her well professionally. "So much carries over from basketball to my job as an FBI agent," says Bates. "Even more than from my law degree. Playing basketball, I learned that with hard work and a willingness to make sacrifices, you can overcome obstacles. I learned how to put differences aside to work with others toward common goals. Those things carry over into everything I do. Most people interviewing me for this job were really impressed that I had played basketball in school. They understand that it takes dedication. You play hurt, you play tired. That conditioned me for a stressful job with long hours.

"It's only recently that women have started to get the respect they deserve in the work place," says Bates. "The same could be said of women in basketball. I don't know of any woman who would want to hear she does a good job 'for a woman.' I can't go out and arrest a 250-pound man on my own. But some men would have a problem with that, as well. I do what is asked of me, and I have proven myself," she says, "and that's where it should end."

Laura Sikes

GROWING UP in Cairo, Georgia, Teresa Edwards spent little time with other girls; they were interested in cheerleading, while she ran in track meets and played softball and basketball. "Whatever the boys did, I did," recalls Edwards. "My mother killed me for it, but I'd go back out every day anyway." In most sports, she just held her ground, but in basketball, she was better than the boys. At twelve, she made the junior high school team. Playing for Cairo High School, she led her team to a state title her senior year.

Offered numerous basketball scholarships, Edwards chose the University of Georgia, where she received her B.S. in recreation in 1989. The intensely competitive 5'11" guard scored a career high of 40 points in a game against Tennessee her senior year; four days later, LSU held her to 12 points, but she managed 15 rebounds, another career high.

Edwards is the University of Georgia's all-time leader in assists (653) and steals (342) and ranks third on the school's all-time scoring records. In her four years, Georgia had a 116-17 record, won three Southeastern Conference championships, and reached the Women's Final Four twice. She is a Kodak All-American and was a gold medalist in the 1984 and 1988 Olympics and the 1987 Pan Am Games.

Six months of the year, Edwards plays on a professional team in Japan. "I feel like a stranger there, but I enjoy basketball so much that I'll play it anywhere," says Edwards, who is the first American guard hired to play on a Japanese team. She admires the Japanese players' quickness and strength as well as their work ethic.

"I've tried to help my teammates get more enjoyment out of our games," she says, "but the Japanese have taught me that it doesn't necessarily have to be fun." She misses American fans and the collegiate atmosphere. "We never had sellouts, but there were always the faithful few who would show up. The fans helped all of us feel good about what we were doing."

She recalls Georgia coach Andy Landers with special admiration. "He was always in charge, and he worked us very hard. Some kids will run from that," she ponders. But not Edwards, who says she would like to be somewhat like him when she turns to college coaching in the coming years.

The members of the
1991 Division I Kodak
All-America Team,
(from left to right, front
row) Sonja Henning,
Dawn Staley, Dana
Chatman, Andrea Stinson,
(back row) Kerry Bascom,
Delmonica DeHorney,
Daedra Charles, Genia
Miller, Joy Holmes,
and Carolyn Jones,
share in a 17-year
tradition of excellence.

Timothy M. McDonough

EACH YEAR since 1975, the Eastman Kodak Company has sponsored five women's All-America basketball teams selected by the Women's Basketball Coaches Association. To choose the players, nine coaches, one from each WBCA district, cast their votes for candidates nominated and elected in district-wide competitions involving every coach in the division. In addition to the Division I team, Kodak sponsors All-America teams for Divisions II and III, NAIA, and Junior/Community Colleges as part of its far-reaching program to support and promote amateur athletics in the United States.

THE IDEA FOR AT THE RIM evolved in a restaurant in Atlanta over duck, chocolate desserts, and a vision of something good for women's athletics, and specifically, for women's basketball. In an effort to acknowledge those who helped craft that vision into this book, the Women's Basketball Coaches Association would like to thank: Eastman Kodak Company Vice-President Raymond H. DeMoulin, without whose unfailing support AT THE RIM would never have been possible; the 1990-91 WBCA Executive Committee, including Kay Yow, North Carolina State; Rene Portland, Penn State University; Jill Hutchison, Illinois State University; Jim Foster of St. Joseph's University; Dianne Nolan, Fairfield University; and Marti Gasser, U.S. Air Force Academy; the WBCA Board of Directors; our corporate board, which includes William D. Brew, Canon USA, Inc.; Donna S. Buchanan, Jack Morton Productions; Karl Flemke, Junior Achievement, Inc.; Robert L. Garretson, A.E. Staley Manufacturing Company; John R. Hansen Hospitality Franchise Systems, Inc.; Judith Eller Street; Lewis Hardy, Champion Products, Inc.; W. James Host, Host Communications; Ilah Merriman, H&R Block of Houston; and Roger Morningstar of Converse, Inc.

Special thanks go to WBCA Communications Specialist Maria Ahmann for her invaluable editorial contributions to this project. Our thanks also go out to all the sports information directors who assisted Leah Painter Roberts, Thomasson-Grant, and the WBCA in obtaining information; and finally, to the coaches of the WBCA, without whose support and commitment to coaching great athletes and better women this book could never have been produced.

Betty F. Jaynes

Jeanie Adams
Bowling Green, Kentucky

Amanda L. Alcock
Chicago Sun Times

Ellen M. Banner
Seattle, Washington

Rebecca Barger
Philadelphia Inquirer

Donna Bagby
Dallas Times Herald

Nicole Bengiveno
Matrix, N.Y., N.Y.

Lois Bernstein
The Sacramento Bee

Susan Biddle
The White House

Paula Bronstein
The Hartford Courant

Christine Cotter
Los Angeles Times

Dana Fineman
Sygma, N.Y., N.Y.

Pat Greenhouse
The Boston Globe

Judy Griesedieck
Hamel, Minnesota

Renee' Hannans
Atlanta Journal-Constitution

Adrienne Helitzer
Pomona, California

Lynn Johnson
Black Star, N.Y., N.Y.

Marlene Karas
Atlanta Journal-Constitution

Pauline Lubens
Detroit Free Press

Paula Nelson
The Dallas Morning News

Mary Schroeder
Detroit Free Press

Mary E. Schulte
Kansas City Star

Callie Shell
The Pittsburgh Press

Jean Shifrin
Atlanta Journal-Constitution

Laura Sikes
Atlanta Journal-Constitution

Meri Simon
San Francisco *Daily
Ledger-Post Dispatch*

Pam Spaulding
Louisville *Courier-Journal*

Barbara M. Trammell
Arlington, Texas

Vicki Valerio
The Philadelphia Inquirer

Lisa Waddell-Buser
Memphis *Commercial Appeal*

Cindy Yamanaka
The Dallas Morning News